JBIOG
Penn
Boothroyd, Jennifer.

William Penn /

William Penn

A LIFE OF TOLERANCE

by Jennifer Boothroyd

Lerner Publications Company • Minneapolis

Photo Acknowledgments

The photos in this book are used with the permission of: © Joseph Sohm;ChromoSohm Inc./CORBIS, p. 4; Admiral Penn, n.d., Society Portrait Collection, The Historical Society of Pennsylvania, p. 6; Library of Congress, pp. 7 (LC-USZ62-106735), 20 (LC-USZC4-12141); © North Wind Picture Archives, pp. 8, 10, 11, 12, 16, 19, 22, 23, 24, 25; William Penn Receiving the Charter of Pennsylvania from Charles II, n.d., Stauffer Collection, The Historical Society of Pennsylvania, p. 14; Reproduced with the permission of the Allison-Shelley Collection, Special Collections Library, the Pennsylvania State University, p. 17; Thomas Holme, A Portraiture of the City Philadelphia in the Province of Pennsylvania, 1683, (Of 610" 1683), The Historical Society of Pennsylvania, p. 18; © Jenny Boothroyd, p. 26.
Front Cover: Library of Congress (LC-USZ62-12218).

Lerner Publications Company
A division of Lerner Publishing Group
241 First Avenue North
Minneapolis, MN 55401 U.S.A.

Website address: www.lernerbooks.com

Words in **bold type** are explained in a glossary on page 31.

Library of Congress Cataloging-in-Publication Data

Boothroyd, Jennifer, 1972–
    William Penn : a life of tolerance / by Jennifer Boothroyd.
      p. cm. – (Pull ahead books)
    Includes bibliographical references and index.
    ISBN-13: 978-0-8225-6387-7 (lib. bdg. : alk. paper)
    ISBN-10: 0-8225-6387-8 (lib. bdg. : alk. paper)
    1. Penn, William, 1644–1718–Juvenile literature. 2. Pioneers–Pennsylvania–Biography–
Juvenile literature. 3. Quakers–Pennsylvania–Biography–Juvenile literature. 4.
Pennsylvania–History–Colonial period, ca. 1600–1775–Juvenile literature. I. Title. II. Series.
F152.2.B66 2007
974.8'02092–dc22   2006003462

Manufactured in the United States of America
1 2 3 4 5 6 – JR – 12 11 10 09 08 07

Table of Contents

4

In the Beginning

Have you ever visited Pennsylvania?
William Penn founded this state.
He wanted a place where people of
different **religions** would be welcome.
William believed in **tolerance**. He
felt that people should be free to have
their own beliefs.

William was born in England in 1644.
His father worked for the king.
William's family was well known.

William's father

William Penn

When he grew up, William studied law. He also joined the navy. But religion interested William the most.

William went to a Quaker gathering like this one.

Freedom of Religion

William went to a country called
Ireland. He heard a man speak about
being a **Quaker**. William had met
Quakers when he was a child.
Quakers believe in peace and
tolerance. William liked the Quakers'
ideas. William became a Quaker.

These Quakers were ordered to go to jail.

William returned to England. Quakers were not free to **worship** in England.

Everyone had to follow the king's religion. It was the law. Many Quakers met in secret.

The king of England

William wrote about being a Quaker. He was sent to jail many times for sharing his beliefs.

William is told he will go to jail.

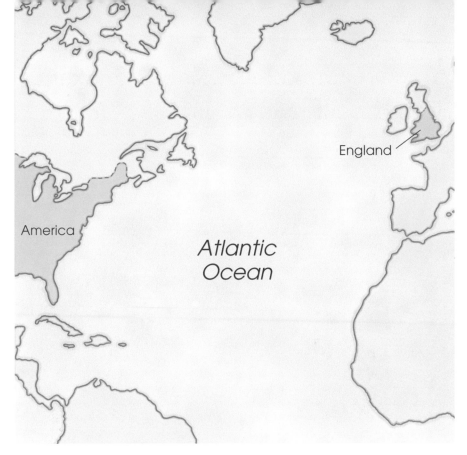

America is across the Atlantic Ocean from England.

William wanted to live in America.
People had more freedom there.

The king gives William land in America.

Welcome to America

The king of England **owed** William's family a lot of money. William asked the king to pay him with land in America. The king gave William some land. The king named the land Pennsylvania. William would lead this **colony**.

William spoke about laws for the colony.

William made the laws for this new land.
His laws allowed people in Pennsylvania
to worship freely.

William told people in other countries about the colony. He asked them to move to Pennsylvania.

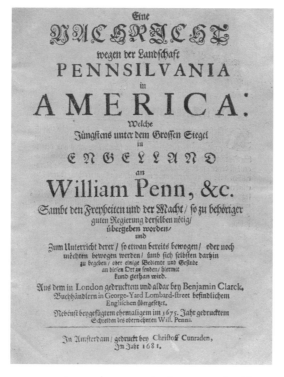

This German poster asks people to move to Pennsylvania.

William carefully planned the city of Philadelphia in Pennsylvania. He wanted it to include parks.

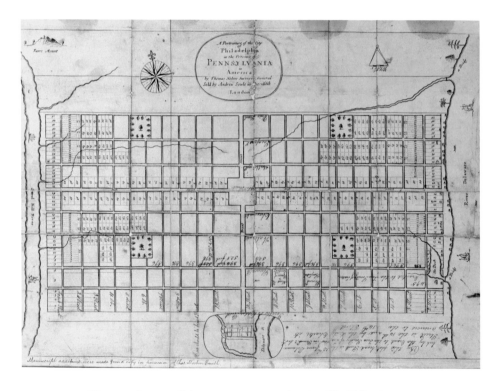

The parks on this map are marked with little trees.

Quakers and people of other religions **settled** in Philadelphia. They lived, worked, and worshiped there.

Many people lived in Pennsylvania before William came.

Native Americans

Native Americans lived in Pennsylvania before the **colonists** came. Most colonists forced Native Americans to leave their land. William did not. He treated the Native Americans with tolerance and **respect**.

William told colonists in Pennsylvania
that they must pay the Native Americans
for their land.

William met with Native American
leaders. They made a written
agreement called a **treaty**.

The treaty explained how the colonists and Native Americans would live together in peace.

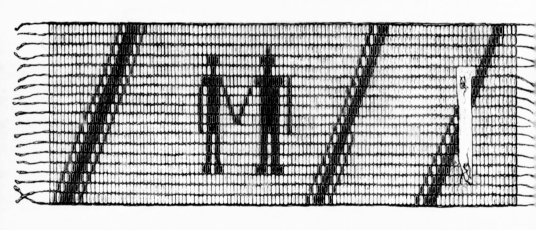

Native Americans gave this weaving to William as a gift.

They agreed to solve any problems
they had together.

This statue of William Penn stands in Philadelphia.

Making a Difference

William Penn's ideas made a difference in history. People in the United States still obey many of the laws he made. But most importantly, William taught people how to live together in peace and tolerance.

WILLIAM PENN TIMELINE

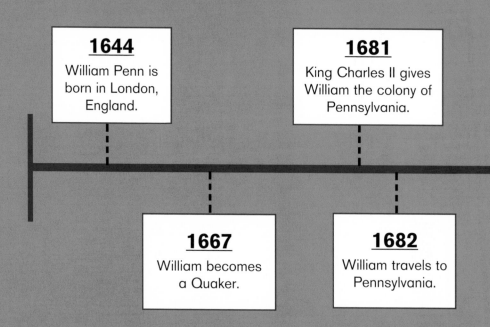

1644
William Penn is born in London, England.

1681
King Charles II gives William the colony of Pennsylvania.

1667
William becomes a Quaker.

1682
William travels to Pennsylvania.

1701

William signs Pennsylvania's constitution, called the Charter of Privileges.

1982

Welcome Park celebrates the 300th anniversary of the founding of Pennsylvania.

1718

William Penn dies in England.

More about William Penn

● The king of England chose the name Pennsylvania–*Penn* for William's father and *Sylvania,* which means "wooded land." William tried to change the colony's name because he didn't want people to think he named it after himself.

● William paid the Native Americans 20 blankets, 50 shirts, kettles, coats, scissors, shoes, combs, and knives for his first piece of land.

● When planning Philadelphia, William wanted many parks and green spaces around the neighborhoods. He hoped this would stop the spread of diseases and fire in the city.

Websites

Pennsbury Manor
http://www.pennsburymanor.org

Pennsylvania Historical and Museum Commission
http://www.phmc.state.pa.us/ppet/penn/page1.asp?
secid=31

Glossary

colonists: people who live in a colony

colony: a group of people living together and ruled by another country

owed: to have to repay something

Quaker: a member of the Religious Society of Friends

religions: belief in God or gods and the traditions of this belief

respect: to treat someone with honor and care

settled: made a place to live

tolerance: accepting people who have beliefs and traditions different from yours

treaty: a written agreement between two or more groups

worship: to honor God or gods

Index